Dr. Jeeva Jose

Customer Payment Trend Analysis based on Clustering for Predicting the Financial Risk of Business Organizations

Anchor Academic
Publishing

Jose, Jeeva: Customer Payment Trend Analysis based on Clustering for Predicting the
Financial Risk of Business Organizations, Hamburg, Anchor Academic Publishing 2017

Buch·ISBN: 978·3·96067·104·6
PDF·eBook·ISBN: 978·3·96067·604·1
Druck/Herstellung: Anchor Academic Publishing, Hamburg, 2017
Covermotiv: © pixabay.de

Bibliografische Information der Deutschen Nationalbibliothek:
Die Deutsche Nationalbibliothek verzeichnet diese Publikation in der Deutschen
Nationalbibliografie; detaillierte bibliografische Daten sind im Internet über
http://dnb.d·nb.de abrufbar.

Bibliographical Information of the German National Library:
The German National Library lists this publication in the German National Bibliography.
Detailed bibliographic data can be found at: http://dnb.d·nb.de

© Anchor Academic Publishing, Imprint der Diplomica Verlag GmbH
Hermannstal 119k, 22119 Hamburg
http://www.diplomica·verlag.de, Hamburg 2017
Printed in Germany

SYNOPSIS

Customer Payment Trend Analysis based on Clustering for Predicting the Financial Risk of Business Organizations

With the opening of Indian economy, many multinationals are shifting their manufacturing base to India. This includes setting up green field projects or acquiring established business firms of India. The region of this business unit is expanding globally. The variety and number of customer base is getting expanded and the business risk related to bad debts is increasing. Close monitoring and analysis of payment trend helps to predict customer behavior and predict the chances of customer financial strength.

The present manufacturing companies generate and store tremendous amount of data. The amount of data is so huge that manual analysis of the data is difficult. This creates a great demand for data mining to extract useful information buried within these data sets. One of the major concerns that affect the company's investment and profitability is bad debts; this can be reduced by identifying past customer behavior and reaching the suitable payment terms.

Objectives

1. Cluster analysis of the credit type base to find the most suitable payment terms.
2. To find the mean number of invoices paid in time, within 30 days (On time), within 60 days, within 90 days and over 90 days as per present payment terms.
3. To find how close the objects in a cluster are using the standard deviation of each attribute values.

The research followed a typical Knowledge Discovery in Data (KDD) framework, where data mining is the core in the whole process. The research went through all the nine steps of KDD. The research design was both exploratory and descriptive. The study was conducted in a FCI's manufacturing facility in Kochi, Kerala. FCI is one of the largest electronic component manufacturers in world having manufacturing and marketing network globally. The duration of this study was six months. There are 1010 customers and 30 payment terms. From these payment terms four were selected for study & analysis.

The billing data, payment data and the corresponding payment ageing report records were collected for a period of six months from the databases of billing section. K-means clustering method to segment the credit terms for business risk prediction model was used in the research.

The Clustering and Prediction module was implemented in WEKA – a free open source software written in java.

Findings

The clustering method identified four clusters based on customer's payment term behavior pattern. The clusters are termed as I000COD, I020BKT, I00000M, I030RRT.

The company can go to customers to revise present payment terms according to the way in which the customers make their payments. The invoicing to customers can be controlled based on due date of payment, when the customers will have a tendency to misuse the payment terms.

The high value for cluster mean for **Cluster 0** is shown for 90 days and above. The standard deviation of this cluster is high for 90 days and above. The inference is that most of the customers belonging to this credit type have a tendency to pay after 90 days and organization can re think of providing this credit type in future. The high value of standard deviation implies that the number of invoices of different customers show a wide variation ranging from 0-50.

The high value for cluster mean for **Cluster 1** is shown for 61-90 days. The standard deviation value of this cluster is high for 61-90 days and lowest for 90 days and above. The inference is that most of the customers belonging to this credit type have a tendency to pay after 60 days and organization can think of changing the credit terms with these customers. The high value of standard deviation implies that the number of invoices of different customers show a wide variation ranging from 0-48.

The high value for cluster mean for **Cluster 2** also is shown for 61-90 days. The standard deviation value of the cluster 2 is also high for 61-90 days. The inference is that most of the customers belonging to this credit type have a tendency to pay after 60 days and organization can think of changing the credit terms with these customers. The high value of standard deviation implies that the number of invoices of different customers show a wide variation ranging from 0-50.

The high value for cluster mean for **Cluster 3** is shown for 0-30 days. The standard deviation values of the cluster 3 is high for 0-30 days .The inference of the study is that this credit term customers (I030RRT – within 30 days of receipt) are most reliable and less risky and highly suitable to the organization in terms of risk of payment risk.

TABLE OF CONTENTS

Chapter 1
INTRODUCTION

1.1 Problem Formulation

This study is done at FCI's manufacturing base at Kochi, Kerala. This manufacturing base is having an annual turnover of 250 million IRs and customer base of 1030 numbers. FCI is one of the largest electronic components manufacturer in world having 40 manufacturing bases scattered in France, Spain, Italy, UK, Ireland, Australia, USA, Canada, Mexico, Japan, Taiwan, China and India. For different customers, the payment terms are selected from the existing 30 types. This is initially fixed based on organization's general reputation, industry feedback etc. Many of the customers are in other continents and chances of right information on the financial condition of these customers reaching FCI may get delayed. Continuous monitoring and analysis of customer payments to be done to see the customer's binding to agreed payment terms will help to foresee the risk and take corrective actions.

Some customers will adhere to payment terms and some will deviate from agreed payment terms. It is necessary to identify the class of customers who deviate from the payment terms on generally so that the specific payment term can be given to future customers in case of absolute necessity as well as for taking actions to change that payment terms of customers who are in that class.

This can be analyzed by clustering techniques. The clustering based on partitioning methods was found suitable for solving this problem. Hence the K-means algorithm which uses the partitioning methods was used in this study.

1.2 Objective

The study is done at FCI Ltd., Kochi. The organization has 30 payment terms which was agreed and created for last several years of business. Some terms are as old as 20 years and some are irreverent in present business scenario. 1000VPM against VPP is an example. Some are very vague and cannot be monitored or controlled correctly. 1000CNC (after completion) is another example. This does not specify the target date and keep the payment receiving date in open. The payment term 1000COD (cheque on delivery) is also very vague and open as it does not specify the date to be mentioned on the cheque. Customers can take this as granted and can issue cheque as per the date they prefer.

Many payment terms are created for single customer. Some payments terms are highly risky and there are many examples of bad debts in past. The payment term risk can be found out by analyzing the past data. The objective of this study is to analyze the payment terms of customers in general and find out the payment term in which most of the customers do not adhere to.

1.3 Scope of the Study

The scope of this study extends to analyzing the customer payment terms set by the company and the risks related to this. The study will help the organization to avoid providing risky payment terms to new customers in future. This will also help management to initiate action or encourage for changing existing customer to opt for some other payment terms.

Chapter 2
REVIEW OF LITERATURE

2.1 Introduction to Clustering

Clustering is the classification of objects into different groups, or more precisely, the partitioning of a data set into subset (clusters), so that the data in each subset (ideally) share some common trait – often proximity according to some defined distance measure. The distance between points in a cluster (inter cluster) is less than the distance between a point in the cluster and any point outside it. Clustering is similar to 'database segmentation' [1].

Clustering has been used in many application domains including biology, medicine, anthropology, marketing and economics. Clustering applications include plant and animal classification, disease classification, image processing, pattern recognition and document retrieval.

2.2 Definition

The clustering problem is stated as follows. Assume that the number of clusters to be created as the input value, k. The actual content of each cluster, K_j , $1<=j<=k$, is determined as a result of the function definition. Without loss of generality, we will view that the result of solving a clustering problem is that a set of clusters is created: $K = \{K_1, K_2, \ldots\ldots, K_k\}$

12

Given a database $D = \{t_1, t_2, ..., t_n\}$ of tuples and an integer value k, the clustering problem is to define a mapping $f : D \longrightarrow (1, 2, ..., k)$ where each t_i is assigned to one cluster K_j, $1<=j<=k$. A cluster, K_j, contains precisely those tuples mapped to it; that is, $K_j = \{t_i | f(t_i) = K_j, 1<=j<=n$ and $t_i \, \varepsilon \, D\}$ [2].

2.3 Need for Data Mining in Organizations

Today's business environment is more competitive than ever. The difference between survival and defeat often rests on a thin edge of higher efficiency than the competition. The advantage is often the result of better information technology providing the basis for improved business decisions. The problem of how to make such business decisions is therefore crucial. One answer is through better analysis of data. Data mining is a methodology to assess the value of the data and to leverage that value as an asset to provide large returns on the analytic investment.

The problem that often confronts researchers new to the field is that there are a variety of data mining techniques available and which one to choose. Some are more difficult to use than others, and they differ in other, superficial ways but most importantly, the underlying algorithms used differ and the nature of these algorithms is directly related to the quality of the results obtained and ease of use.

Some estimates hold that the amount of information in the world doubles every twenty years. In 1989, the total number of databases in the world was estimated at five million, most of which were small local computer files [4]. Today the automation of business transactions produces a large amount of data because even simple transactions like telephone calls, shopping trips, medical tests and consumer product warranty registrations are recorded in a computer. Scientific databases are also growing rapidly. NASA, for example, has more data that it can analyze. The 2000 US census data of over a billion bytes contains an untold quantity of hidden patterns that describe the lifestyles of the population [5]. Most of this data will never be seen by human beings and even if viewed could not be analyzed by hand.

Byte magazine reported that some companies have reaped returns on investment of as much as 1000 times their initial investment on a single project. More and more companies are realizing that the massive amounts of data that they have been collecting over the years can be their key to success. With the proliferation of data warehouses, this data can be mined to uncover the hidden nuggets of knowledge. Data mining tools are fast becoming a business necessity. The Gartner group has predicted that data mining will be one of the five hottest technologies in the early years of the new century.

There are currently several data mining techniques available. Not all of these are equal in effectiveness. Data mining is widely used in business, science and military applications. Data mining can allow an organization to market customers on an individual or household basis, selecting those are most likely to be responsive and suggesting targeted creative messages.

Data mining is the process of using analytic methods to explore data to discover meaningful patterns that enable organizations to operate in a more cost effective manner. It brings out linear relationships and can handle noisy or incomplete data. It can also model large numbers of variables which is useful in modeling purchase transactions, click stream data or gene problems. Data mining uses powerful new rule induction technology to make explicit relationships in both numeric and nonnumeric data.

There are non data mining methods like query tools with graphical components. Some tools support a degree of multi-dimensionality such as cross tab reporting, time series analysis, drill down, slice, dice and pivoting. These tools are sometimes a good adjunct to data mining tools in that they allow the analyst an opportunity to get a feel for the data. They can help to determine the quality of the data and which variables might be relevant for a data mining project to follow. They are useful for further explore the results supplied by true data mining tools. These approaches have several limitations. Querying is effective only when the investigation is limited to a relatively small number of known questions.

2.4 Data Mining Methods

a) Statistical methods

There are several statistical methods used in data mining projects that are widely used in science and industry that provide excellent features for describing and visualizing large chunks of data. Some of the methods commonly used are regression analysis, correlation, discriminant analysis, hypothesis testing and prediction [6]. This is a first step for good understanding of data. These methods deal well with numerical data where the underlying probability distributions of the data are known. They are not as good with nominal or binary data [7].

Statistical methods require statistical expertise, or a project person well versed in statistics who is heavily involved. Such methods require difficult to verify statistical assumptions and do not deal well with non-numeric data. They suffer from black box aversion syndrome. This means that non-technical decision makers, those who will either accept or reject the results of the study, are often unwilling to make important decisions based on a technology that gives them answers but does not explain how it got the answers. To tell a non-statistician CEO that he or she must make a crucial business decision because of a favourable R statistic is not usually well received.

Another problem is that statistical methods are valid only if certain assumptions about the data are met. Some of these assumptions are linear relationships between pairs of variables, nonmulticolinearity, normal probability distributions and independence of samples. If we do not validate these assumptions because of time limitations or are not familiar with them, our analysis may be faulty and therefore the results may not be valid.

b) Neural Networks

This is a popular technology, particularly in the financial community. This method was originally developed in the 1940s to model biological nervous systems in an attempt to mimic thought processes. The end result of a neural net project is a mathematical model of the process. It deals primarily with numerical attributes but not as well with nominal data [8].

There is still much controversy regarding the efficacy of neural nets. One major objection to the method is that the development of a neural net model is partly an art and partly a science in that results often depend on the individual who built the model. The model called network topology may differ from one researcher to another for the same data. There is the problem that often occurs of over fitting that results in good prediction of the data used to build the model but bad results with new data.

c) Decision Trees

Decision tree methods are techniques for partitioning a training file into a tree representation [9]. The starting node is called the root node. Depending upon the results of a test, this node is then partitioned into two or more subsets. Each node is then further partitioned until a tree is built. This tree can be mapped into a set of rules. Fairly fast and results can be presented as rules.

The most important negative for decision trees is that they are forced to make decisions along the way based on limited information that implicitly leaves out of consideration the vast majority of potential rules in the training file. This approach may leave valuable rules undiscovered since decisions made early in the process will preclude some good rules from being discovered later.

2.5 Types of Business Models

There are several business models in data mining which are used in industries.

a) Claims Fraud Models

The number of challenges facing the property and casualty insurance industry seems to have grown geometrically during the past decade. In the past, poor underwriting results and high loss ratio were compensated by excellent returns on investments. However, the performance of financial markets today is not sufficient to deliver the level of profitability that is necessary to support the traditional insurance business model. In order to survive in the bleak economic conditions that dictate the terms of today's merciless and competitive market, insurers must change the way they operate to improve their underwriting results and profitability. An important element in the process of defining the strategies that are essential to ensure the success and profitable results of insurers is the ability to forecast the new directions in which claims management should be developed. This endeavor has become a crucial and challenging undertaking for the insurance industry, given the dramatic events of the past years in the insurance industry worldwide. We can check claims as they arrive and score them as to the likelihood of they are fraudulent. This can results in large savings to the insurance companies that use these technologies [10].

b) Customer Clone Models

The process for selectively targeting prospects for your acquisition efforts often utilizes a sophisticated analytical technique called "best customer cloning." These models estimate which prospects are most likely to respond based on characteristics of the company's "best customers". To this end, we build the models or demographic profiles that allow you to select only the best prospects or "clones" for your acquisition programs. In a retail environment, we can even identify the best prospects that are close in proximity to your stores or distribution channels. Customer clone models are appropriate when insufficient response data is available, providing an effective prospect ranking mechanism when response models cannot be built [10].

c) Response Models

The best method for identifying the customers or prospects to target for a specific product offering is through the use of a model developed specifically to predict response. These models are used to identify the customers most likely to exhibit the behavior being targeted. Predictive response models allow organizations to find the patterns that separate their customer base so the organization can contact those customers or prospects most likely to take the desired action. These models contribute to more effective marketing by ranking the best candidates for a specific product offering thus identifying the low hanging fruit [10].

d) Revenue and Profit Predictive Models

Revenue and Profit Prediction models combine response/non-response likelihood with a revenue estimate, especially if order sizes, monthly billings, or margins differ widely. Not all responses have equal value, and a model that maximizes responses doesn't necessarily maximize revenue or profit. Revenue and profit predictive models indicate those respondents who are most likely to add a higher revenue or profit margin with their response than other responders [10].

These models use a scoring algorithm specifically calibrated to select revenue-producing customers and help identify the key characteristics that best identify better customers. They can be used to fine-tune standard response models or used in acquisition strategies.

e) Cross-Sell and Up-Sell Models

Cross-sell/up-sell models identify customers who are the best prospects for the purchase of additional products and services and for upgrading their existing products and services. The goal is to increase share of wallet. Revenue can increase immediately, but loyalty is enhanced as well due to increased customer involvement [10].

f) Attrition Models

Efficient, effective retention programs are critical in today's competitive environment. While it is true that it is less costly to retain an existing customer than to acquire a new one, the fact is that all customers are not created equal. Attrition models enable you to identify customers who are likely to churn or switch to other providers thus allowing you to take appropriate preemptive action. When planning retention programs, it is essential to be able to identify best customers, how to optimize existing customers and how to build loyalty through "entanglement". Attrition models are best employed when there are specific actions that the client can take to retard cancellation or cause the customer to become substantially more committed. The modeling technique provides an effective method for companies to identify characteristics of consumers for acquisition efforts and also to prevent or forestall cancellation of customers [10].

g) Marketing Effectiveness Creative Models

Often the message that is passed on to the customer is the one of the most important factors in the success of a campaign. Models can be developed to target each customer or prospect with the most effective message. In direct mail campaigns, this approach can be combined with response modeling to score each prospect with the likelihood they will respond given that they are given the most effective creative message (i.e. the one that is recommended by the model). In email campaigns this approach can be used to specify a customized creative message for each recipient [10].

h) Real Time Web Personalization with eNuggets

Using eNuggets real time data mining system websites can interact with site visitors in an intelligent manner to achieve desired business goals. This type of application is useful for e-commerce and CRM sites. eNuggets is able to transform Web sites from static pages to customized landing pages, built on the fly, that match a customer profile so that the promise of true one-to-one marketing can be realized [10].

eNuggets is a revolutionary new business intelligence tool that can be used for web personalization or other real time business intelligence purposes. It can be easily integrated with existing systems such as CRM, Outbound telemarketing (i.e. intelligent scripting), insurance underwriting, stock forecasting, fraud detection, genetic research and many others.

eNuggets uses historical (either from company transaction data or from outside data) data to extract information in the form of English rules understandable by humans. The rules collectively form a model of the patterns in the data that would not be evident to human analysis. When new data comes in, such as a stock transaction from ticker data, eNuggets interrogates the model and finds the most appropriate rule to suggest which course of action will provide the best result (i.e. buy, sell or hold) [10].

2.6 Classification of Clusters and Clustering Techniques

A classification of the different types of clustering algorithms can be shown in the following Figure 2.1.

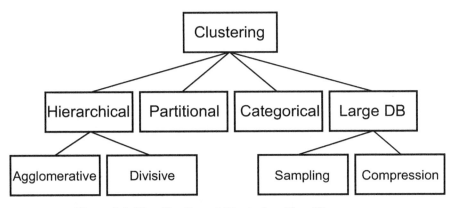

Figure 2.1 Classification of Clustering Algorithm

Clustering algorithm themselves may be viewed as hierarchical or partitional. With hierarchical clustering a nested set of clusters is created. Each level in the hierarchy has a separate set of clusters. At the lowest level, each item is in its unique cluster. At the highest level, all items belong to the same cluster. With partitional clustering, the algorithm creates only final set is created. Traditional clustering algorithms tent to be targeted to small numeric databases that fit into memory. There is however more recent clustering algorithms that look at the categorical data and are targeted to larger, perhaps dynamic, databases. Algorithms targeted to larger databases may adapt to memory constraints either sampling the database or using data structures, which can be compressed or pruned to fit into memory regardless of the size of the database. Clustering algorithms may also differ based on whether they produce overlapping or non-overlapping cluster. Even though we consider only non-overlapping clusters, it is possible to place an item in multiple clusters. Non-overlapping clusters can be viewed as intrinsic or extrinsic. Extrinsic technique use labelling of the items to assist in the classifications process. These algorithms are the traditional classification supervised learning algorithms in which a special input training set is used. Intrinsic algorithms do not use any a priority category labels, but dependent only on the adjacency matrix containing the distance between objects [1]. All algorithms examine here is the intrinsic class.

2.7 Similarity and Distance Measures

There are many desirable properties for the clusters created by a solution to a specific clustering problem. The most important one is that a tuple within one cluster is more like tuples within that cluster that it is similar to tuples outside it. As with classification then, assume the definition of a similarity measure, $sim(t_i, t_l)$ defined between ant two tuples, t_i, t_l ε D. This provides a stricter and alternative clustering definition as follows.

Given a database $D=\{ t_1, t_2, ..., t_n \}$ of tuples, a similarity measure, $sim(t_i, t_l)$, defined between any two tuples, $t_i, t_l \ \varepsilon \ D$, and an integer value k, the clustering problem is to define a mapping $f : D\{1, 2, ..., k\}$ where each t_i is assigned to one cluster K_j, $1 <= j <= k$. Given a cluster, K_j, $\forall \ t_{jl}, t_{jm} \ \varepsilon \ K_j$ and $t_i \ \varepsilon \ K_j$, $sim(t_{jl}, t_{jm}) > sim(t_{jl}, t_i)$.

A distance measure, $dis(t_{jl}, t_{jm})$, as opposed to similarity, is often used in clustering. Some clustering algorithms look only at numeric data, usually assuming metric data points. Metric attributes satisfy the triangular inequality. The clusters can then be described by using several characteristic values.

2.8 Representation of Clustering

Clustering can be considered the most important *unsupervised learning* problem; so, as every other problem of this kind, it deals with finding a *structure* in a collection of unlabeled data. A loose definition of clustering could be "the process of organizing objects into groups whose members are similar in some way". A *cluster* is therefore a collection of objects which are "similar" between them and are "dissimilar" to the objects belonging to other clusters. This can be shown with a simple graphical example as in Figure 2.2.

In this case we easily identify the 4 clusters into which the data can be divided; the similarity criterion is distance: two or more objects belong to the same cluster if they are "close" according to a given distance (in this case geometrical distance). This is called distance-based clustering. Another kind of clustering is conceptual clustering: two or more objects belong to the same cluster if this one defines a concept common to all that objects. In other words, objects are grouped according to their fit to descriptive concepts, not according to simple similarity measures.

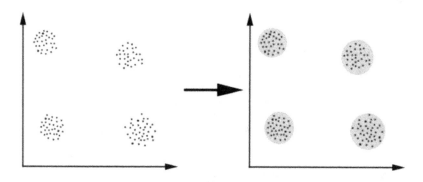

Figure 2.2 Representation of Clusters

2.9 Goal of Clustering

The goal of clustering is to determine the intrinsic grouping in a set of unlabeled data. But how to decide what constitutes a good clustering? It can be shown that there is no absolute "best" criterion which would be independent of the final aim of the clustering. Consequently, it is the user which must supply this criterion, in such a way that the result of the clustering will suit their needs. For instance, we could be interested in finding representatives for homogeneous groups (*data reduction*), in finding "natural clusters" and describe their unknown properties (*"natural" data types*), in finding useful and suitable groupings (*"useful" data classes*) or in finding unusual data objects (*outlier detection*).

2.10 Examples of Clustering Application

- Marketing: Help marketers discover distinct groups in their customer bases, and then use this knowledge to develop targeted marketing programs.
- Land use: Identification of areas of similar land use in an earth observation database.
- Insurance: Identifying groups of motor insurance policy holders with a high average claim cost.
- City-planning: Identifying groups of houses according to their house type, value, and geographical location.
- Earth-quake studies: Observed earth quake epicenters should be clustered along continent faults.

Chapter 3
METHODOLOGY

3.1 Partitioning Method

There exists a large number of clustering algorithms. The choice of clustering algorithm depends on type of data available and on the particular purpose and application. The method used to identify the clusters in this research is the partitioning method.

Given a database of n objects or data tuples, a partitioning method constructs k-partitions of the data, where each partition represents a cluster and k<=n. that is it classifies the data into k groups which together satisfies the following requirements.

1. Each group must contain at least one object.
2. Each object must belong to exactly one group.

Given k, the number of partitions to construct, a partitioning method creates an initial partitioning. It then uses an iterative relocation technique that attempts to improve the partitioning by moving objects from one group to another. The general criterion of a good partitioning is that objects in the same cluster are close or related to each other whereas objects of different clusters are far apart or very different. There are various kinds of other criteria for judging the quality of partitions.

To achieve global optimality in partitioning based clusterring would require the exhaustive enumeration of all possible partitions. Most applications adopt one of two popular heuristic methods [1].

1. K-means algorithm, where each cluster is represented by the mean value of the objects in the cluster.

2. K-medoids algorithm, where each cluster is represented by one of the objects located near the center of the cluster. These heuristic clustering methods work well for finding spherical-shaped clusters in small to medium sized databases. To find clusters with complex shapes and for clustering very large data sets, partitioning methods need to be extended.

In this research, K-means algorithm is used for clustering as it was found most suitable.

3.2 K-means Algorithm for Partitioning

The K-means algorithm is based on centroid technique. The K-means algorithm takes the input parameter k, and partitions a set of n objects into k clusters so that the intra cluster similarity is high but the inter cluster similarity is low. Cluster similarity is measured in regard to the mean value of the objects in a cluster, which can be viewed as the cluster's center of gravity.

The K-means algorithm proceeds as follows. First it randomly selects k objects, each of which initially represents a cluster mean or center. For each of the remaining objects, an object is assigned to the cluster to which it is most similar based on the distance between the object and the cluster mean. It then computes the new mean for each cluster. This process iterates until the criterion function converges. Typically, the squared error criterion is defined as

$$E= \sum_{i=1}^{k} \sum_{p \in C_i} |p-m_i|^2$$

Where E is the sum of square-error for all objects in the database, p is the point in space representing a given object, and m_i is the mean of the cluster C. This criterion tries to make the resulting k clusters as compact and as separate as possible. The algorithm attempts to determine k partitions that minimize the squared error criterion function. It works well when the clusters are compact clouds that are rather well separated from one another.

The method is relatively scalable and efficient in processing large datasets because the computational complexity of the algorithm is O(nkt), where n is the total number of objects, k is the number of clusters and t is the number of iterations. Normally k<<n and t<<n. The method often terminates at a local optimum.

The K-means method can be applied only when the mean of a cluster is defined. This may not be the case in some applications such as when data with categorical attributes are involved. There are a few quite variants of the K-means method. These can differ in the selection of the initial K-means, calculation of dissimilarity and the strategies for calculating cluster means.

Another variant to K-means is the K-modes method, which extends K-means paradigm to cluster categorical data by replacing the means of clusters with modes, using new dissimilarity measures to deal with categorical objects. And using a frequency based method to update modes of clusters. The K-means and the K-modes methods can be integrated to cluster data with mixed numeric and categorical values resulting in the k-prototypes method.

The EM (Expectation Maximization) algorithm extends the K-means paradigm in a different way. Instead of assigning each object to a dedicated cluster, it assigns each object to a cluster according to a weight representing the probability of membership. In other words there are no strict boundaries between clusters.

The K-means algorithm can be scaled based on the idea of identifying three kinds of regions in data: regions that are compressible, regions that must be maintained in the main memory and regions that are discardable.

a) An object is "discardable" if its membership in a cluster is ascertained.

b) An object is compressible if it is not discardable but belongs to a tight sub cluster

c) A data structure known as "clustering feature is used to summarize objects that have been discarded or compressed.

d) If an object is neither discardable nor compressible, then it should be retained in the main memory.

To achieve scalability, the iterative clustering algorithm only includes the clustering features of the compressible objects and the objects must be retained in main memory, thereby turning a secondary memory based algorithm into a main memory based algorithm.

3.3 Platform Specification

WEKA (Waikato Environment for Knowledge Analysis) is a popular suite of machine learning software written in Java, developed at the University of Waikato. WEKA is free software available under the GNU General Public License [11].

The GNU General Public License (GNU GPL or simply GPL) is a widely used free software license, originally written by Richard Stallman for the GNU project. It is the license used by the Linux kernel. The GPL is the most popular and well known example of the type of strong copyleft license that requires derived works to be available under the same copyleft. Under this philosophy, the GPL is said to grant the recipients of a computer program the rights of the free software definition and uses copyleft to ensure the freedoms are preserved, even when the work is changed or added to. This is in distinction to permissive free software licenses, of which the BSD licenses are the standard examples.

The GNU Lesser General Public License (LGPL) is a modified, more permissive, version of the GPL, intended for some software libraries. There is also a GNU Free Documentation License, which was originally intended for use with documentation for GNU software, but has also been adopted for other uses, such as the Wikipedia project.

Weka is a collection of machine learning algorithms for data mining tasks. The algorithms can either be applied directly to a dataset or called from your own Java code. Weka contains tools for data pre-processing, classification, regression, clustering, association rules, and visualization. It is also well-suited for developing new machine learning schemes.

The Weka workbench contains a collection of visualization tools and algorithms for data analysis and predictive modeling, together with graphical user interfaces for easy access to this functionality. The original non-Java version of Weka was a TCL/TK front-end to (mostly third-party) modeling algorithms implemented in other programming languages, plus data preprocessing utilities in C, and a make file based system for running machine learning experiments. This original version was primarily designed as a tool for analyzing data from agricultural domains, but the more recent fully Java-based version (Weka 3), for which development started in 1997, is now used in many different application areas, in particular for educational purposes and research.

Weka supports several standard data mining tasks, more specifically, data preprocessing, clustering, classification, regression, visualization, and feature selection. All of Weka's techniques are predicated on the assumption that the data is available as a single flat file or relation, where each data point is described by a fixed number of attributes (normally, numeric or nominal attributes, but some other attribute types are also supported). Weka provides access to SQL databases using Java Database Connectivity and can process the result returned by a database query. It is not capable of multi-relational data mining, but there is separate software for converting a collection of linked database tables into a single table that is suitable for processing using Weka. Another important area that is currently not covered by the algorithms included in the Weka distribution is sequence modeling.

Weka's main user interface is the *Explorer*, but essentially the same functionality can be accessed through the component-based *Knowledge Flow* interface and from the command line. There is also the *Experimenter*, which allows the systematic comparison of the predictive performance of Weka's machine learning algorithms on a collection of datasets [12]. Figure 3.1 shows the interface of Weka.

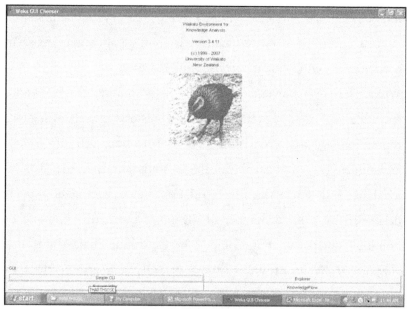

Figure 3.1 Weka Interface

The *Explorer* interface has several panels that give access to the main components of the workbench. The *Preprocess* panel has facilities for importing data from a database, a CSV file, etc., and for preprocessing this data using a so-called *filtering* algorithm. These filters can be used to transform the data (e.g., turning numeric attributes into discrete ones) and make it possible to delete instances and attributes according to specific criteria. The *Classify* panel enables the user to apply classification and regression algorithms (indiscriminately called *classifiers* in Weka) to the resulting dataset, to estimate the accuracy of the resulting predictive model, and to visualize erroneous predictions, ROC curves, etc., or the model itself (if the model is amenable to visualization like, e.g., a decision tree). The *Associate* panel provides access to association rule learners that attempt to identify all important interrelationships between attributes in the data. The *Cluster* panel gives access to the clustering techniques in Weka, e.g., the simple K-means algorithm. There is also an implementation of the expectation maximization algorithm for learning a mixture of normal distributions. The next panel, *Select attributes* provides algorithms for identifying the most predictive attributes in a dataset. The last panel, *Visualize*, shows a scatter plot matrix, where individual scatter plots can be selected and enlarged, and analyzed further using various selection operators.

Chapter 4
ANALYSIS AND DESIGN

According to Han and Kamber [1], the nine steps of Knowledge discovery from data are

1. Learning the application domain
2. Creating target data set: data selection
3. Data cleaning and preprocessing
4. Data reduction and transformation
5. Choosing functions of data mining
6. Choosing the mining algorithms
7. Data mining
8. Pattern Evaluation and knowledge presentation
9. Use of discovered knowledge

4.1 Learning the Application Domain

The customer's payment terms are initially fixed on the basis of the organization general reputation, feedback from other sources etc. The customers are supposed to pay in correct time as per the agreed payment terms. A grace period of 30 days is allowed considering the payment processing at customer end, postal delays, bank transfer delays etc. If a customer enjoys the 30 days grace period for majority all of their payments, this will be considered as a purposeful activity and actions will be taken for revising the payment terms. In case customers cross the credit limit within this time frame automatically credit hold is implemented. Further billing to this customer can be done only after opening the hold. The GM-Marketing holds the authority to open the credit hold based on discussion with customer and company finance controller.

If a customer is not paying within 30 days, the specific non paid invoices are traced separately and actions will be taken to settle that. Also, if the total amount exceeds the credit limit, these customers are put in "Credit hold". A customer who pays majority of invoices between 30-60 days was analyzed and actions were taken to revise the payment terms.

If invoices are getting paid after 60 days, it is considered as a risky business or customer. Legal proceedings will be initiated, if payments are due after 90 days.

4.2 Creating Target Data Set

From a total of 1010 customers and 59 payment types 98.16 % customers falls within four payment terms. They are I000COD, I020BKT, I00000M and I030RRT. I000COD means Cash/Cheque/DD on delivery. 1020BKT means "Documents through bank". I00000M means against delivery. I030RRT means within 30 days of receipt. All selected payment terms is of assured payment within 30 days. The corresponding payment detail records are collected for a period of six months January 2006 to June 2006.

4.3 Data Cleaning and Preprocessing

There are a number of data preprocessing techniques. Data Cleaning can be applied to remove noise and correct inconsistencies in the data. The methods for data preprocessing is organized into the following categories.

1. Data cleaning
2. Data integration
3. Data transformation
4. Data reduction

Data cleaning routines work to clean the data by filling in missing values, smoothing noisy data, identifying or removing outliers and resolving inconsistencies. Dirty data can cause confusion for the mining procedure, resulting in unreliable output. Although most mining routines have some procedures for dealing with incomplete or noisy data, they are not always robust. Instead they may concentrate on avoiding over fitting the data to the function being modeled. Therefore a useful preprocessing step is to run the data through some data cleaning routines.

Data integration combines data from multiple sources into a coherent data store as in data warehousing. These sources may include multiple databases, data cubes or flat files. The various issues in data integration are

1. Entity identification problem
2. Redundancies
3. Detection and resolution of data value conflicts.

Redundancies can be detected by correlation analysis. Careful integration of the data from multiple sources can help reduce and avoid redundancies and inconsistencies in the resulting data set. This can improve the accuracy and speed of the subsequent data mining process.

Since the percentage of customers using following payment terms form a major part, only these payment terms are considered for analysis. Table 4.1 shows the various payment terms and the percentage of customers.

Payment Type	Percentage of Customers
I000COD	26.62%
I020BKT	21.38%
I00000M	25.54%
I030RRT	24.15%
Others	**1.84%**

Table 4.1: Payment Terms (Credit Types) and Percentage of Customers

4.4 Data Reduction and Transformation

In data transformation, the data are transformed or consolidated into forms appropriate for mining. Data transformation can involve the following.

a) Smoothing – which works to remove the noise data.

b) Aggregation – where summary or aggregation operations are applied to the data.

c) Generalization of the data – where low-level data are replaced by higher level concepts through the use of concept hierarchies.

d) Normalization – where the attribute data are scaled so as to fall within a small specified range such as -1.0 to 1.0 or 0.0 to 1.0.

e) Attribute construction – where new attributes are constructed and added from the given set of attributes to help the mining process.

Data reduction techniques can be applied to obtain a reduced representation of the data set that is much smaller in volume, yet closely maintains the integrity of the original data. That is mining on the reduced data set should be more efficient yet produce the same analytical results.

Strategies for data reduction include the following.

a) Data cube aggregation – where aggregation operations are applied to the data in the construction of a data cube.

b) Dimension reduction – where irrelevant, weakly relevant or redundant attributes or dimensions may be detected and removed.

c) Data compression – where encoding mechanisms are used to reduce the data set size.

d) Numerosity Reduction – where the data are replaced or estimated by alternative, smaller data representations such as parametric models or non parametric methods such as clustering, sampling and the use of histograms.

e) Discretization and concept hierarchy generation – where raw data values for attributes are replaced by ranges or higher conceptual levels. Concept hierarchies allow the data mining at multiple levels of abstraction and are a powerful tool for data mining.

4.5 Identification of the Fields for the Study

Variables/Information not significant to study was filtered out. From a total of 20 fields, from different types of information shown in the table, only 5 fields were selected for the study. Those fields were credit type, Number of invoices paid within 30 days, Number of invoices paid after 30 days and within 60 days, No. of invoices paid after 60 days and within 90 days and No. of invoices paid after 90 days or Number of invoices paid after legal proceedings. Table 4.2 shows the different variables used for data mining.

Sl. No.	Variables
1	Credit Type
2	No. of Invoices paid within 30 days
3	No. of Invoices paid after 30 days and within 60 days
4	No. of Invoices paid after 60 days and within 90 days
5	No. of Invoices paid after 90 days

Table 4.2: Variables used for Data Mining

The other fields such as customer name, invoice date, payment date, region of customer, Sales person, invoice value, credit limit, discount etc. were filtered as these does not come under the scope of study.

4.6 K-Means Algorithm

The K-means algorithm for partitioning based on the mean value of the objects in the cluster.

Input: The number of clusters k and a database containing n objects.

Output: A set of k clusters that minimizes the squared error criterion.

Method:

1. Arbitrarily choose k objects as the initial cluster centers.
2. Repeat
3. (re)assign each object to the cluster to which the object is most similar, based on the mean value of the objects in the cluster;
4. update the cluster means, i.e, calculate the mean value of the objects for each cluster;
5. until no change

Chapter 5
IMPLEMENTATION RESULTS AND DISCUSSION

The raw data was obtained from the finance Department of FCI, Cochin. The data was extracted from their Enterprise Resource Planning Package MFG PRO. The data was captured to various worksheets in MS-Excel. The data after cleaning, transformation, integration and reduction was saved on a new MS-Excel Worksheet. The MS- Excel Worksheet was saved as a CSV file because WEKA can interpret only files saved in certain formats like CSV. The following Figure 5.1 shows the input CSV file.

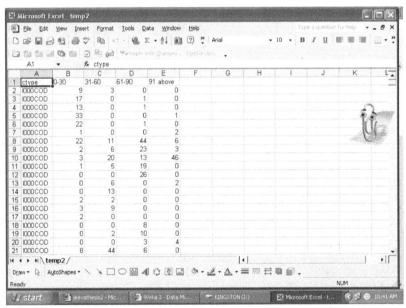

Figure 5.1 Input CSV File

The above said CSV file was given as input to Weka Explorer shown in Figure 5.2.

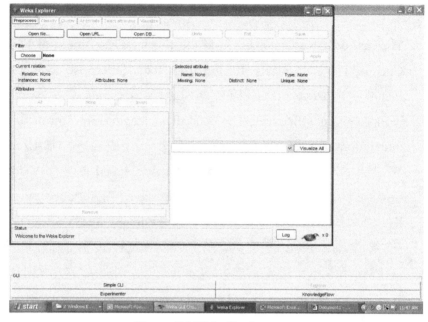

Figure 5.2 Weka Explorer

This explorer is used for implementing the K-means algorithm and to generate the clusters. In addition to the generation of clusters, the cluster mean and standard deviation values for each cluster was also generated. The mean value for each attribute like number of invoices paid within 30 days, number of invoices paid after 30 days and within 60 days, number of invoices paid after 60 days and within 90 days and number of invoices paid after 90 days or number of invoices paid after legal proceedings were also displayed.

Similarly the standard deviation for the each above said attribute was also generated in order to predict how close the objects in a cluster are close to each other. The Table 5.1 shows the various clusters and the standard deviations.

CLUSTER 0 (I000COD)

No. of Days	0-30	31-60	61-90	90 above
Cluster Mean	6.3198	5.2267	5.5872	6.7965
Standard Deviation	10.3414	9.6694	9.5916	10.8109

CLUSTER 1 (I030RRT)

No. of Days	0-30	31-60	61-90	90 above
Cluster Mean	6.4304	5.8734	6.7025	5.538
Standard Deviation	10.7231	9.1698	11.0405	8.993

CLUSTER 2 (I00000M)

No. of Days	0-30	31-60	61-90	90 above
Cluster Mean	6.3174	5.988	7.1916	6.2814
Standard Deviation	9.7382	9.308	10.6295	8.5573

CLUSTER 3 (I020BKT)

No. of Days	0-30	31-60	61-90	90 above
Cluster Mean	8.5286	6.1714	7.15	6.6143
Standard Deviation	12.5638	9.5163	11.4715	10.3927

Table 5.1 Clusters and Standard Deviations

Using the Weka Explorer, the number of clusters was set to 4 and an initial seed was set to 4. The following Figure 5.3 shows the input form for setting the number of clusters and initial seed.

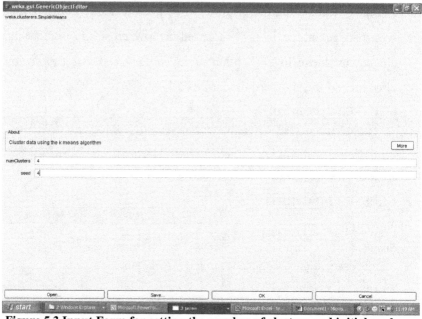

Figure 5.3 Input Form for setting the number of clusters and initial seed

The result was as follows shown in Figure 5.4.

Figure 5.4 Output Window of Various Clusters

1. Four clusters namely I000COD, I020BKT, I00000M, I030RRT was generated.
2. Along with that the mean value for each delay period was also generated.
3. The standard deviation showing for each delay period was also generated.

The Histogram representation of the total number of invoices in different credit types was also generated which is shown in Figure 5.5.

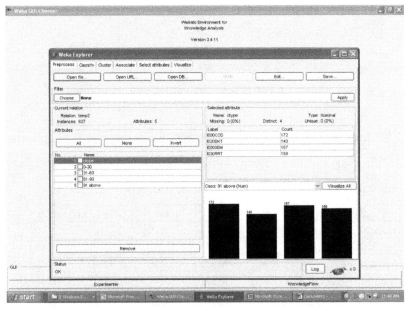

Figure 5.5 Histogram Representation of Various Credit Types

The period wise histogram representation was also generated and is shown in Figure 5.6.

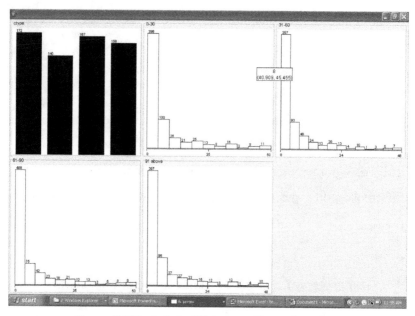

Figure 5.6 Periodwise Histogram Representation

The number of invoices paid within various periods, maximum
number of invoices, mean value for the number of invoices and
standard deviation are shown in Table 5.2.

Period in Days	0-30	31-60	61-90	Above 90
MINIMUM	0	0	0	0
MAXIMUM	50	48	50	48
MEAN	6.832	5.794	6.628	6.309
STANDARD DEVIATION	10.826	9.404	10.654	9.713

Table 5.2 Number of Invoices paid within various periods

The various credit types available and their description in raw data
is demonstrated in Table 5.3.

Sl. No.	Credit Types	Description
1	6	C.O.D basis
2	150	90% through bank & balance after receipt
3	15d	15 days D/A through Bank
4	I00000C	100% thru CDA (R&D) HYBD
5	I00000M	Against delivery
6	I00030C	30% advance & balance after acceptance.
7	I00050C	50% advance & balance after completion.
8	I00090C	90% on receipt & balance within 30 days.
9	I00095C	95% on receipt & balance within 30 days.
10	I000ADC	Advance Payment Received
11	I000AIC	After acceptance of item
12	I000AOT	100% advance with order
13	I000ATT	Advance TT
14	I000CNC	After completion
15	I000COD	Cheque On Delivery
16	I000DIC	On delivery & installation.
17	I000DOD	D/D On Delivery
18	I000LCT	Against LC AT SIGHT
19	I000PRC	Against Performa Invoice
20	I000RRC	Immediately on receipt of item
21	I000SMC	Free Samples
22	I000VPM	Against VPP
23	I00150C	15% advance & balance on COD
24	I01090C	90% within 10 days, balance in 30 days.
25	I010RRT	Within 10 days of Receipt
26	I01500T	Within 15 days of Invoice Date
27	I015PDC	15 days PDC on COD Basis
28	I015RRT	Within 15 days of Receipt.
29	I020BKT	Against document through Bank
30	I021PDC	21 days PDC on COD Basis
31	I03000C	30 days PDC on COD Basis
32	I03000T	Within 30 days of invoice date
33	I030ASI	Within 30 days after Submission of Invoice
34	I030DAT	30 days Documents through bank.
35	I030LCT	30 days L/C
36	I030PDC	30 days PDC
37	I030RRT	Within 30 days of receipt.
38	I030WBT	Within 30days from despatch
39	I035DAT	35 days after acceptance
40	I04500C	45 days PDC on COD Basis
41	I04500T	45 days from date of Invoice

42	I045LCT	45 days L/C
43	I045PDC	45 days PDC
44	I045RRT	Within 45 days of Receipt.
45	I06000T	Within 60 days of invoice date
46	I060DAT	60 days D/A through Bank
47	I060DTT	Direct
48	I060LCT	60 days L/C
49	I060PDC	60 days PDC on COD Basis
50	I060RRT	Within 60 days of Receipt.
51	I09000T	90 days from date of Invoice
52	I090AD&I	90% Against delivery & 10% after Installation
53	I090DAT	90 days Documents through bank
54	I090LCT	Letter of Credit
55	I090RRT	90 days on receipt of item
56	I090TLC	100% 90 days Usance LC
57	I12000T	120 days from date of invoice
58	I150CST	As per consignment stock agreement
59	I4560PC	50% 45 days PDC, 50% 60 days PDC

Table 5.3 Credit Types and their Description

Source Code

The source code for generating the clusters using Weka is given below.

```
/*Simple K-Means.java*/

package weka.clusterers;
import java.io.*;
import java.util.*;
import weka.core.*
import weka.filters.Filter;
import
weka.filters.unsupervised.attribute.ReplaceMissingVa
lues;
import weka.experiment.Stats;
```

```java
import weka.classifiers.rules.DecisionTable;

public class SimpleKMeans extends Clusterer
implements NumberOfClustersRequestable,
OptionHandler,WeightedInstancesHandler{
private ReplaceMissingValues m_ReplaceMissingFilter;
private m_NumClusters=4
private Instances m_ClusterCentrioids;
private Instances m_ClusterStdDevs;
private int[][] m_ClusterNominalCounts;
private int[] m_Clustersizes;
private int m_Seed=10;
private double[]m_Min;
private double[]m_Max;
private int m_Iterations=0;
private double[] m_squaredErrors;
public String globalInfo(){
return "Cluster data using the k-means algorithm";
}

public void buildClusterer(Instances data) throws
Exception{
m_Iterations=0;
if(data.checkForStringAttributes()){
throw new Exception("Can't handle string
attributes!");
}

m_ReplaceMissingFilter=new ReplaceMissingValues();
Instances instances=new Instances(data);
```

```
instances.setClassIndex(-1);
m_ReplaceMissingFilter.setInputFormat(instances);
instances=Filter.useFilter(instances,m_ReplaceMissin
gFilter);

m_Min=new double[instances.numAttributes()];
m_Max=new double[instances.numAttributes()];
for(int i=0;i<instances.numAttributes();i++)
{
m_Min[i]=m_Max[i]=Double.NaN;
}

m_ClusterCentroids=new
Instances(instances,m_NumClusters);
int[]clusterAssignments=new
int[instances.numInstances()];

for(int i=0;i<instances.numInstances();i++)
{
updateMinMax(instances.instance(i));
}

random RandomO=new Random(m_Seed);
int instIndex;
HashMap initC=new HashMap();
DecisionTable.hashKey hk=null;

for(int j=instances.numInstances()-1;j>=0;j--)
{instIndex=RandomO.nextInt(j+1);
```

```
hk=new
DecisionTable.hashKey(instances.instance(instIndex),
instances.numAttributes(),true);
if(!initC.containsKey(hk))
{
m_ClusterCentroids.add(instances.instance(instIndex)
);
initC.put(hk,null);
}
instances.swap(j,instIndex);

if(m_ClusterCentroids.numInstances()==m_NumClusters)
{
break;
}
}

m_NumClusters=m_ClusterCentroids.numInstances();

int i;
boolean converged=false;
int emptyClusterCount;
Instances[]tempI=new Instances[m_NumClusters];
m_squaredErrors=new double[m_numClusters];
m_ClusterNominalCounts= new int
[m_NumClusters][instances.numAttributes()][0];

while(!converged){
emptyClusterCount=0;
m_Iterations++;
```

```
converged=true;
for(i=0;i<instances.numInstances();i++)
{
Instance toCluster=instances.instance(i);
int newC=clusterProcessedInstance(toCluster,true);

if(newC!=clusterAssignments[i]){
converged=false;
}
clusterAssignments[i]=newC;
}

//update centroids
m_ClusterCentroids=new
Instances(instances,m_NumClusters);
for(i=0;i<m_NumClusters;i++)
{
temp[i]=new Instances(instances,0);
}

for(i=0;i<instances.numInstances();i++)
{
tempI[clusterAssignments[i]].add(instances.instance(
i));
}

for(i=0;i<m_NumClusters;i++)
{
double[]vals=new double[instances.numAttributes()];
if(tempI[i].numInstances()==0){
```

```
//empty cluster
emptyClusterCount++;
}
else
{
for(int j=0;j<instances.numAttributes();j++)
{
vals[j]=tempI[i].meanOrMode(j);
m_ClusterNominalCounts[i][j]=tempI[i].attributeStats
(j).nominalCounts;
}
m_ClusterCemtroids.add(new Instance(1.0,vals));
}
}

if(emptyClusterCount>0)
m_NumClusters-=emptyClusterCount;

tempI=new Instances[m_NumClusters];
}
if(!converged)
{
m_squaredErrors=new double[m_NumClusters];
m_ClusterNominalCounts=new
int[m_NumClusters][instances.numAttributes()][0];
}
}

m_ClusterStdDevs=new
Instances(instances,m_NumClusters);
```

```
m_ClusterSizes=new int[m_NumClusters];
for(i=0;i<m_NumClusters;i++)
{
double[]vals2=new double[instances.numAttributes()];
for(int j=0;j<instances.numAttributes();j++)
{
if(instances.attribute(j).isNumeric())
{
vals2[j]=Math.sqrt(tempI[i].variance(j));
}
else
{
vals2[j]=Instance.missingValue();
}
}
m_ClusterStdDevs.add(new Instance(1.0,vals2));
m_ClusterSizes[i]=tempI[i].numInstances();
}
}

private      int      clusterProcessedInstance(Instance
instance,boolean updateErrors){
double minDist=Integer.MAX_VALUE;
int bestCluster=0;
for(int i=0;i<m_NumClusters;i++)
{
double
dist=distance(instance,m_ClusterCentroids.instance(i
));
if(dist<minDist)
```

```
{
minDist=dist;
bestCluster=i;
}
}
if(updateErrors)
{
m_squaredErrors[bestCluster]+=minDist;
}
return bestCluster;
}


public int clusterInstance(Instance instance) throws
Exception
{
m_ReplaceMissingFilter.input(instance);
m_ReplaceMissingFilter.batchFinished();
Instance inst=m_ReplaceMissingFilter.output();

return clusterProcessedInstance(inst,false);
}


private double distance(Instance first, Instance
second)
{
double distance=0;
int firstI,secondI;
```

```
for(int
p1=0,p2=0;p1<first.numValues()||p2<second.numValues(
);)
{
if(p1>=first.numValues())
{
firstI=m_ClusterCentroids.numAttributes();
}
else
{
firstI=first.index(p1);
}
if(p2>=second.numValues())
{
secondI=m_ClusterCentroids.numAttributes();
}
else
{
secondI=second.index(p2);
}

double diff;
if(firstI==secondI)
{
diff=difference(firstI,first.valueSparse(p1),second.
valueSparse(p2));
p1++;
p2++;
}
else if(firstI>secondI)
```

```
{
diff=difference(secondI,0,second.valueSparse(p2));
p2++;
}
else
{
diff=difference(firstI,first.valueSparse(p1),0);
p1++;
}
distance+=diff*diff;
}
return distance;
}


private  double  difference(int  index,  double
val1,double val2)
{
switch(m_ClusterCentroids.attribute(index).type())
{
case Attribute.NOMINAL:
      if(Instance.isMissingValue(val1)||
         Instance.isMissingValue(val2)||
((int)val1!=(int)val2))
{
return 1;
}
else
{
return 0;
}
```

```
case Attribute.NUMERIC:
        if(Instance.isMissingValue(val1)||
           Instance.isMissingValue(val2))
{

        if(Instance.isMissingValue(val1)&&
           Instance.isMissingValue(val2))
{ return 1;
}
else
{
double diff;
if(Instance.isMissingValue(val2))
{
diff=norm(val1,index);
}
else
{
diff=norm(val2,index);
}
if(diff<0.5)
{
diff=1.0-diff;
}
return diff;
}
}
else
{
return norm(val1,index)-norm(val2,index);
```

```
}
default:
return 0;
}
}

private double norm(double x,int i)
{
if(Double.isNaN(m_Min[i])||Utils.eq(m_Max[i],m_Min[i
]))
{
return 0;
}
else
{
return(x-m_Min[i]/m_Max[i]-m_Min[i]);
}
}

private void updateMinMax(Instance instance)
{
for(int
j=0;j<m_ClusterCentroids.numAttributes();j++)
{
if(!instance.isMissing(j)){
if(Double.isNaN(m_Min[j])){
m_Min[j]=instance.value(j);
m_Max[j]=instance.value(j);
}
else
```

```java
{
if(instance.value(j)<m_Min[j])
{
m_Min[j]=instance.value(j);
}
else
{
if(instance.value(j)>m_Max[j])
{
m+Max[j]=instance.value(j);
}
}
}
}
}
}

public int numberOfClusters() throws Exception{
return m_NumClusters;
}
public Enumeration listOptions()
{
Vector newVector=new Vector(2);

newVector.addElement(new      Option("\tnumber      of
clusters.(default=2).",
                  "N",1,"-N<num>"));
newVector.addElement(new    Option("\trandom    number
seed.\n(default 10)",
                  "S",1,"-S<num>"));
```

```java
return newVector.elements();
}


public String numClustersTipText(){
return "set number of clusters";
}


public void setNumClusters(int n) throws Exception{
if(n<=0)
{
throw new Exception("Number of clusters must be>0");
}
m_NumClusters=n;
}


public int getNumClusters(){
return m_NumClusters;
}


public String seedTipText()
{
return "random number seed";
}


public void setSeed(int s)
{
m_Seed=s;
}
public int getSeed()
{
```

```
return m_Seed;
}

public void setOptions(String[] options) throws
Exception{

String optionString=Utils.getOption('N',options);
if(optionString.length()!=0)
{
setNumClusters(Integer.parseInt(optionString));
}

optionString=Utils.getOption('S',options);

if(optionString.length()!=0)
{
setSeed(Integer.parseInt(optionString));
}
}

public String[] getOptions(){
String[] options=new String[4];
int current=0;

options[current++]="-N";
options[current++]=""+getNumClusters();
options[current++]="-S";
options[current++]=""+getSeed();
while(current<options.length)
{
```

```java
options[current++]="";
}
return options;
}
public String toString()
{
  int maxWidth=0;
for(int i=0;i<m_NumClusters;i++)
for(int
j=0;j<m_ClusterCentroids.numAttributes();j++)
{
if(m_ClusterCentroids.attribute(j).isNumeric()){
double
width=Math.log(Math.abs(m_ClusterCentroids.instance(
i).value(j)))
Math.log(10.0);
width+=1.0;
if((int)width>maxWidth){
maxWidth=(int)width;
}
}
}
}
StringBuffer temp= new StringBuffer();
String naString="N/A";
for(int i=0;i<maxWidth+2;i++)
{
naString+=" ";
}
```

```
temp.append("\nKMeans\n==========\n");
temp.append("\nNumber                          of
iterations:"+m_Iterations+"\n");
temp.append("Within Cluster sum of squared errors:"+
Utils.sum(m_squaredErrors));

temp.append("\n\nCluster centroids:\n");
for(int i=0;i<m_NumClusters;i++)
{
temp.append("\nCluster"+i+"\n\t");
temp.append("Mean/Mode:");
for(int
j=0;j<m_ClusterCentroids.numAttributes();j++)
{
if(m_ClusterCentroids.attribute(j).isNominal())
{
temp.append(""+m_ClusterCentroids.attribute(j).

value(int)m_ClusterCentroids.instance(i).value(j)));
}
else
{
temp.append(""+Utils.doubleToString(m_ClusterCentroi
ds
              .instance(i).value(j),maxWidth+5,4));
}
}
temp.append("\n\tStd Devs: ");
for(int j=0;j<m_ClusterStdDevs.numAttributes();j++)
{
```

```java
if(m_ClusterStdDevs.attribute(j).isNumeric()){
temp.append(""+Utils.doubleToString(m_ClusterDevs.
             instance(i).value(j),maxWidth+5,4));
}
else
{
temp.append(""+naString);
}
}
}
temp.append("\n\n");
return temp.toString();
}


public Instances getClusterCentroids()
{
return m_ClusterCentroids;
}


public Instances getClusterStandardDevs(){
return m_ClusterStdDevs;
}
 public int[][][] getClusterNominalCounts(){

return m_ClusterNominalCounts;
}


public double getSquaredError(){
return Utils.sum(m_squaredErrors);
}
```

```java
public int[] getClusterSizes(){
return m_ClusterSizes;
}

/*Main Method for testing this class*/

public static void main(String argv[])
{
try{
System.out.println(ClusterEvaluation.
    evaluateClusterer(new SimpleKMeans(),argv));
}
catch(Exception e){
System.out.println(e.getMessage());
e.printStackTrace();
}
}
}
```

Chapter 6
CONCLUSION AND SCOPE FOR FURTHER ENHANCEMENTS

The clustering method identified four clusters based on customer's payment term behavior pattern. The clusters are termed as I000COD, I020BKT, I00000M and I030RRT.

The company can go to customers to revise present payment terms according to the way in which the customers make their payments. The invoicing to customers can be controlled based on due date of payment, when the customers will have a tendency to misuse the payment terms.

The high value for cluster mean for **Cluster 0 (I000COD)** is shown for 90 days and above. The standard deviation of this cluster is high for 90 days and above. The inference is that most of the customers belonging to this credit type have a tendency to pay after 90 days and organization can re think of providing this credit type in future. The high value of standard deviation implies that the number of invoices of different customers how a wide variation ranging from 0-50.

The high value for cluster mean for **Cluster 1 (I020BKT)** is shown for 61-90 days. The standard deviation values of this cluster are high for 61-90 days and lowest for 90 days and above. The inference is that most of the customers belonging to this credit type have a tendency to pay after 60 days and organization can think of changing the credit terms with these customers. The high value of standard deviation implies that the number of invoices of different customers show a wide variation ranging from 0-48.

The high value for cluster mean for **Cluster 2 (I00000M)** also is shown for 61-90 days. The standard deviation values of the cluster 2 are also high for 61-90 days. The inference is that most of the customers belonging to this credit type have a tendency to pay after 60 days and organization can think of changing the credit terms with these customers. The high value of standard deviation implies that the number of invoices of different customers show a wide variation ranging from 0-50.

The high value for cluster mean for **Cluster 3 (I030RRT)** is shown for 0-30 days. The standard deviation values of the cluster 3 is high for 0-30 days .The inference of the study is that the credit term customers (I030RRT – within 30 days of receipt)are most reliable and less risky and highly suitable to the organization in terms of risk of payment risk.

The study is done at an electronic component manufacturing industry. This can be extended to all organization who bills to customers and receive payment which includes tele-communication, wholesale business, service industry, hotel and air lines sector, tourism etc.

BIBLIOGRAPHY

1. Jiawei Han and Micheline Kamber, Data mining concepts and techniques, Morgan Kaufmann Publishers, 2005.

2. Margaret H. Dunham, Data Mining – Introductory and Advanced Topics, Pearson Education India, 2006

3. Ian H Witten and Eibe Frank, Data Mining: Practical Machine Learning Tools and Techniques, Morgan Kaufmann Publishers, Second Edition, 2005.

4. Cornelius T. Leondes, Database and Data Communication Network Systems, Academic Press, 2002.

5. http://www.data-mine.com/white-papers-articles/new-technology/

6. A. Paneerselvam, Research Methodology, Prentice Hall of India Private Limited, New Delhi, 2005, Second Re-Print

7. Johnson, R.A. and G.K. Bhattacharyya, Statistics: Principles and Methods, John Wiley & Sons, New York, 1996.

8. Igor Aleksander and Helen Morton, An Introduction to Neural Computing, International Thomson Computer Press, 1995.

9. J.R. Quinlan, Generating production Rules from Decision Trees, IJCAI, 1987, pp. 304-307.

10. http://www.data-mine.com/white-papers-articles/data-mining-model-types

11. www.cs.waikato.ac.nz/ml/weka

12. www.the-data-mine.com/bin/view/Software/Weka

www.ingramcontent.com/pod-product-compliance
Lightning Source LLC
LaVergne TN
LVHW052312060326
832902LV00021B/3834